The Little Spanish

Coloring Book

by Anna Pomaska

Dover Publications, Inc.
New York

The Little Spanish ABC Coloring Book is a new work,
first published by Dover Publications, Inc., in 1988.

International Standard Book Number: 0-486-25614-6

Manufactured in the United States of America
Dover Publications, Inc.
31 East 2nd Street
Mineola, N.Y. 11501

The Little Spanish ABC Coloring Book

Avión

Bruja

Casa

CH

Chaqueta

Dinero

Elefante

Flor

Gato

Helado

Iglesia

Jirafa

Kimono

ABC

Libro

Lluvia

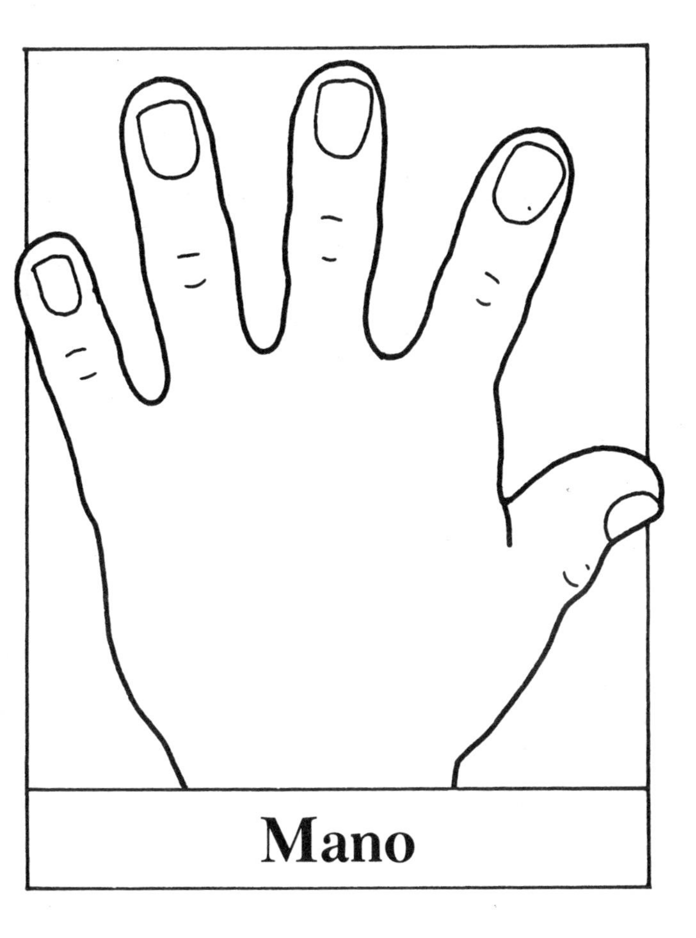
Mano

Niños

Ñu

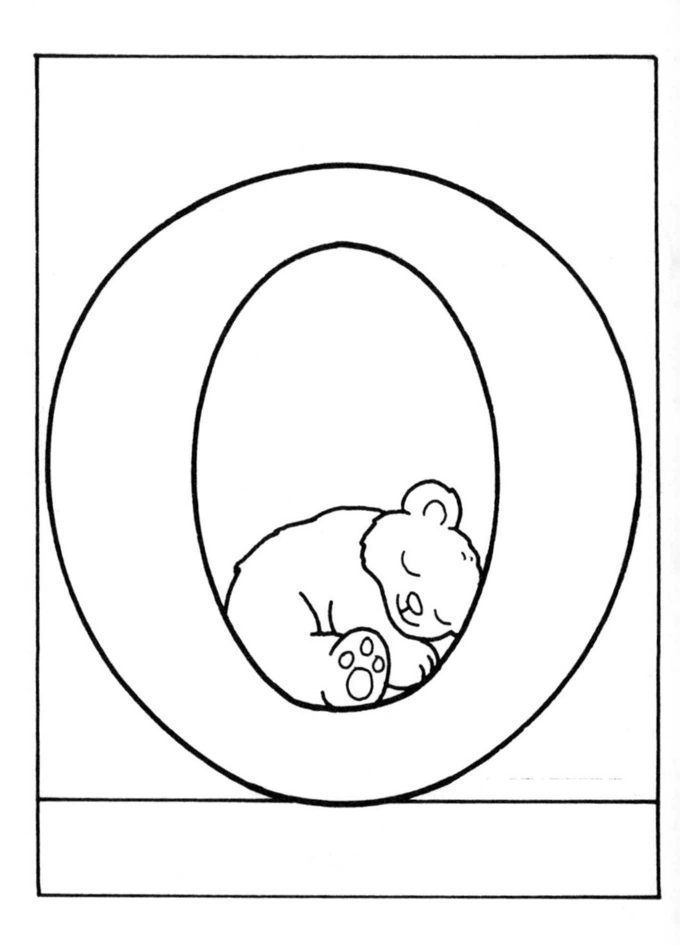

Oso

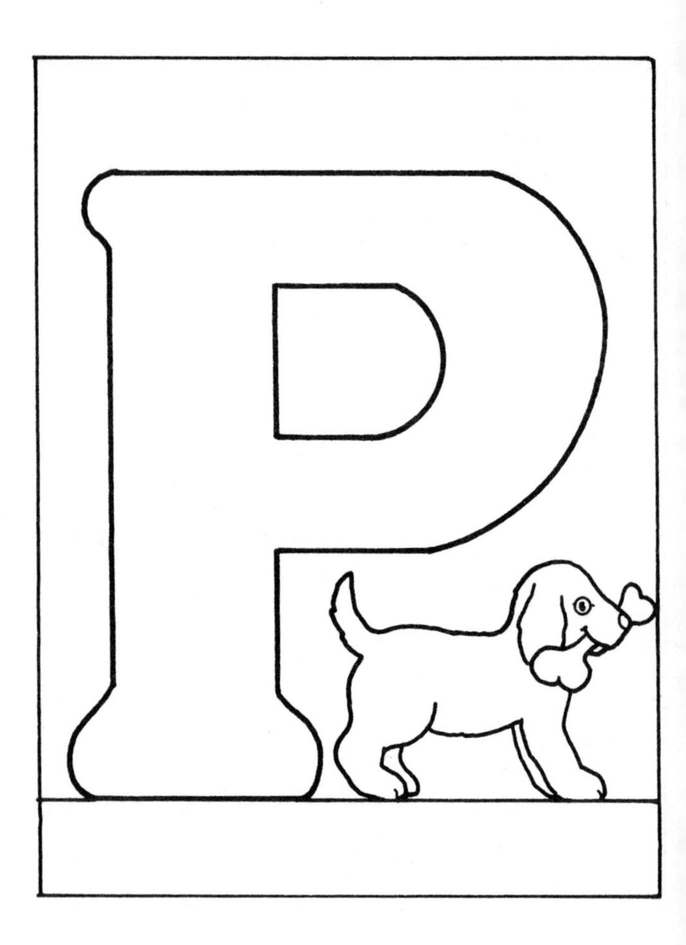

Perro

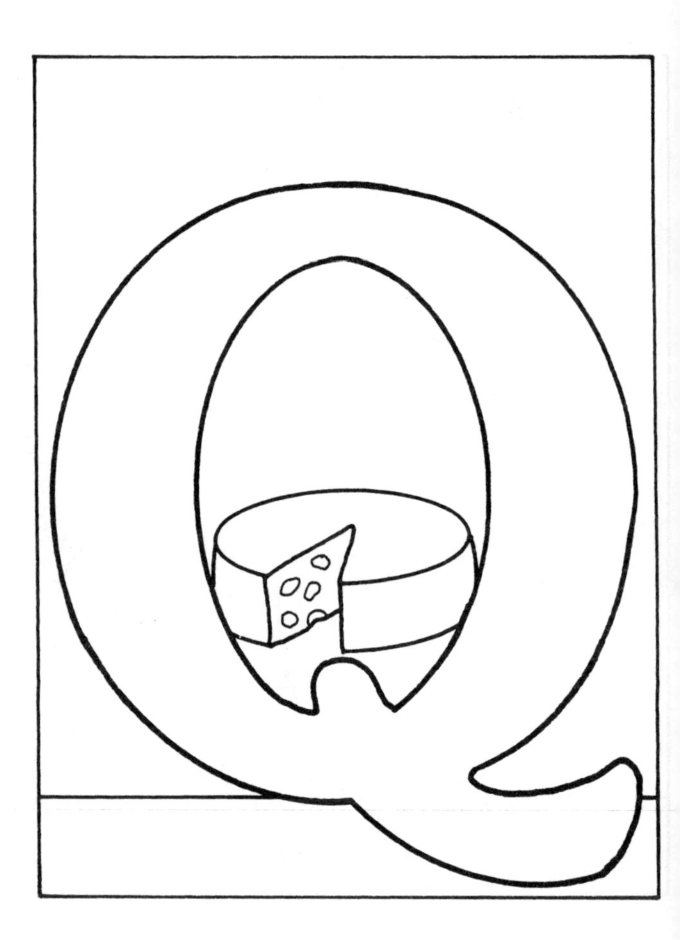

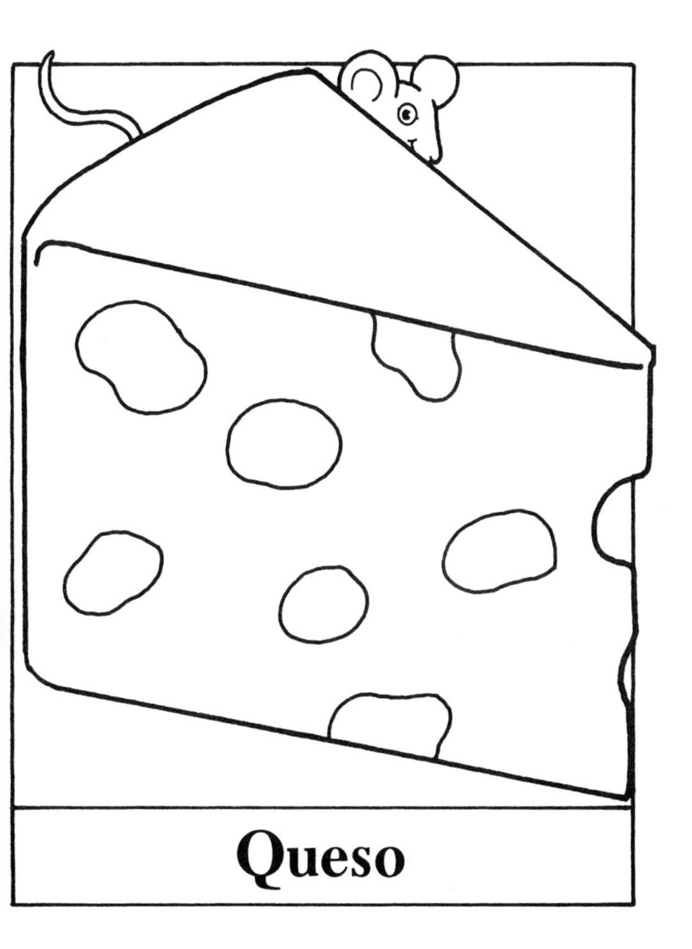
Queso

Ratón

Sol

Tigre

Unicornio

Vaca

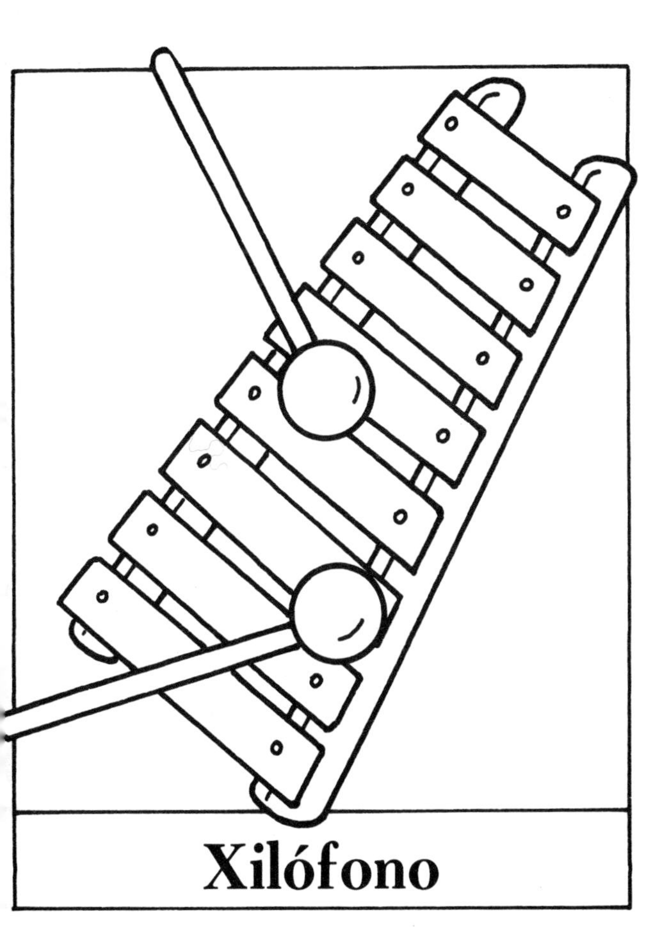

Xilófono

Yak

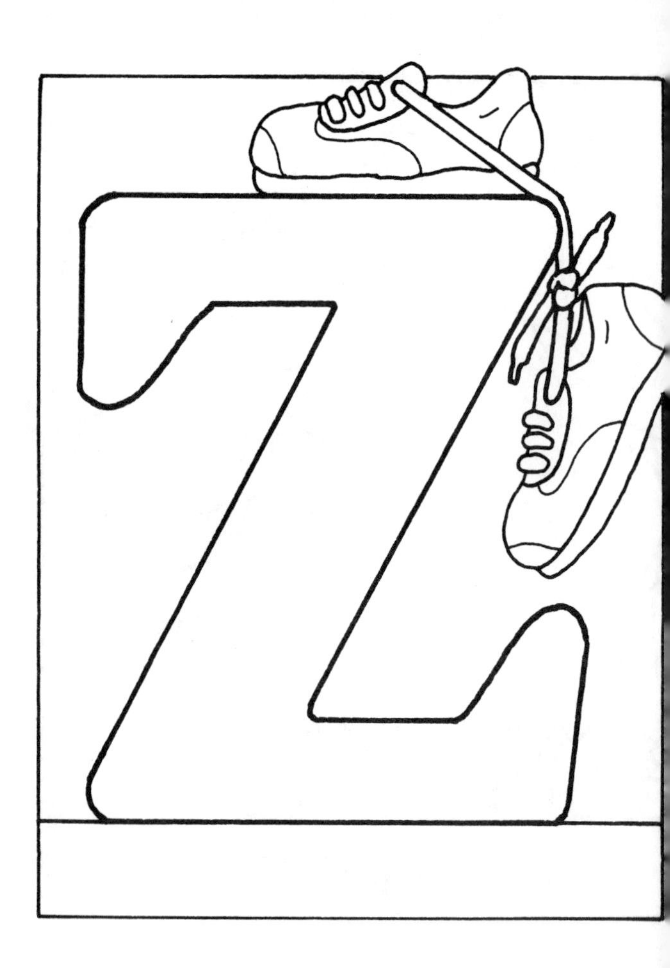

Zapatos

Note

WHETHER CHILDREN ARE studying Spanish as a first or as a second language, they need to learn the alphabet and acquire useful vocabulary. One of the most pleasurable ways to help them remember the letters and new words is by activity, especially in the form of coloring. The present book contains a full Spanish alphabet* keyed to essential everyday words, to names of animals or to concepts that appeal to children ("witch," "unicorn"), all charmingly illustrated. To help children "think in Spanish," only the Spanish words for the items illustrated appear in the main part of the book. On the next two pages the full word list is repeated, not only with the English equivalents (forming a handy glossary) but also with the gender-indicating definite articles, which ideally should be learned right along with the words.

*The letter *w* is omitted as it appears only in clearly non-Spanish words not fully integrated into the language.

Spanish–English Word List

el avión	the airplane
la bruja	the witch
la casa	the house
la chaqueta	the jacket
el dinero	the money
el elefante	the elephant
la flor	the flower
el gato	the cat
el helado	the ice cream
la iglesia	the church
la jirafa	the giraffe
el kimono*	the kimono
el libro	the book
la lluvia	the rain
la mano	the hand
los niños	the children
el ñu	the gnu

el oso	the bear
el perro	the dog
el queso	the cheese
el ratón	the mouse
el sol	the sun
el tigre	the tiger
el unicornio	the unicorn
la vaca	the cow
el xilófono**	the xylophone
el yak	the yak
los zapatos	the shoes

* Also spelled *quimono.*

** Another form in use is *xilofón.*